All About

THE ANCIENT EGYPTIAN PYRAMIDS

Brenda and Brian Williams

Raintree is an imprint of Capstone Global Library Limited, a company incorporated in England and Wales having its registered office at 7 Pilgrim Street, London, EC4V 6LB – Registered company number: 6695582

www.raintreepublishers.co.uk
myorders@raintreepublishers.co.uk

First published in 2008 as Reach for the Stars: Ancient Egyptian Pyramids

This edition © Capstone Global Library Limited 2014

The moral rights of the proprietor have been asserted.

Editorial: Louise Galpine and Claire Throp
Design: Richard Parker and Tinstar Design (www.tinstar.co.uk)
Illustrations: Steve Weston, Sebastian Quigley, International Mapping
Picture Research: Mica Brancic
Production: Victoria Fitzgerald

Originated by Capstone Global Library Ltd
Printed and bound in China by CTPS

ISBN 978 1 406 28580 2 (hardback)
18 17 16 15 14
10 9 8 7 6 5 4 3 2 1

British Library Cataloguing in Publication Data
A full catalogue record for this book is available from the British Library.

Acknowledgements

We would like to thank the following for permission to reproduce photographs: Ancient Art & Architecture Collection Ltd p. 25 (R Sheridan); The Bridgeman Art Library Nationality/Egyptian National Museum, Cairo, Egypt p. 23; Corbis pp. 6–7 (Staffan Widstrand), 8 (Jose Fuste Raga), 9, 14 (Gianni Dagli Orti), 19 (Bojan Brecelj), 21 (Sandro Vannini); Getty Images/Photographer's Choice p. 4 (Daryl Benson); Getty Images/Photographer's Choice/Travelpix Ltd p. 18; Getty Images/Time & Life Pictures/Mansell p. 26; The Kobal Collection/Universal p. 27; The Trustees of the British Museum pp. 16, 17.

Cover photograph of the pyramids Mycerinus, Chephren, and Cheops at Giza, reproduced with permission of Lonely Planet Images/Anders Blomqvist.

We would like to thank Nancy Harris and Kate Spence for their invaluable help in the preparation of this book.

Contents

Some words are printed in bold, **like this**. You can find out what they mean on page 30. You can also look in the box at the bottom of the page where they first appear.

Egypt's pyramids

Just look! They're so big! They are like mountains, but built by people. They are **pyramids**. A pyramid is a shape with a square base. It has four triangular sides. Pyramids seem to point to the stars.

Egyptian fact!

St Paul's Cathedral is in London, England. A cathedral is a large church. It would fit inside the Great Pyramid.

This picture shows the three pyramids at Giza (see map). The Great Pyramid is the big one in the middle.

archaeologist   person who digs in the ground to find out about the past
pyramid   solid shape with a square base and four triangular sides

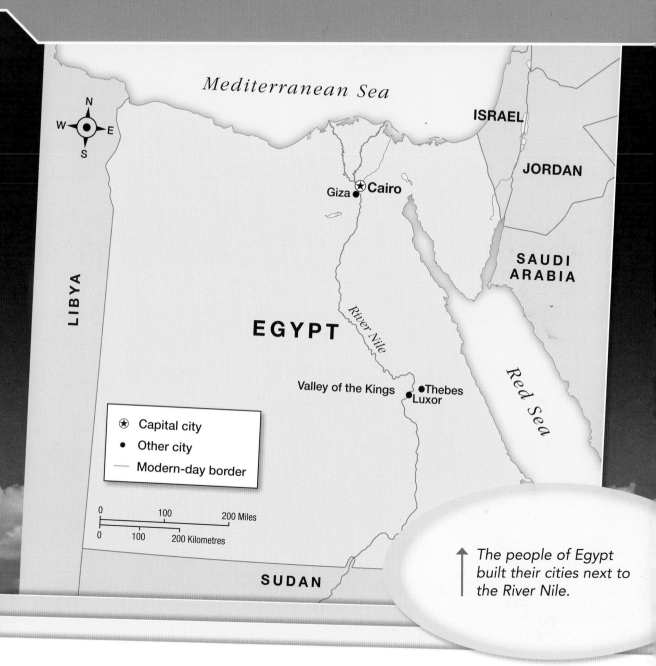

The people of Egypt built their cities next to the River Nile.

The Great Pyramid is made of stones. It is in the country of Egypt. It has stood here for 4,500 years. **Archaeologists** have explored inside and outside the Great Pyramid. They have found clues to how a pyramid was built.

The river floods

Every year, the River Nile rose. Water flowed over the riverbanks. Fields were covered by water. Houses were like islands. But the people of Egypt were happy to see the flood.

People checked how high the Nile flood rose every year. They set up tall stones along the riverbank. They marked on the stone where the water stopped.

The water soon fell again. Black mud was left behind by the flood. The mud was good for growing **crops**. Farmers got busy planting. They could not live without the river.

crops plants grown for food
temple building in which people worship a god or gods

Black and Red Lands

The people of Egypt called their land the "Black Land". They called the desert the "Red Land".

The people of ancient Egypt were farmers. Many Egyptians today are also farmers.

People in ancient Egypt (4,500 years ago) were also builders. They built **pyramids**. They built **temples**. Temples are buildings where people can worship gods. They looked at the Sun, Moon, and stars.

The king commands

Egypt's king was called the pharaoh. In Egypt, the king was a god. People believed he made the Nile flood. People also believed in the **afterlife**. They thought that when a person died, they moved on to another life. This was called an afterlife.

This is a **statue** of the head of the pharaoh Ramesses. It is at the **Temple** of Luxor in Thebes.

afterlife world of the dead
statue figure made from stone or metal
tomb place in which dead people are buried

People put clay models, like this one of an Egyptian farmer, inside a tomb with the dead body.

When a king died, he went to join the other gods. He needed a special **tomb**. A tomb is a place where people are buried. It was called a **pyramid**. Building a pyramid took a long time. King Khufu began his pyramid soon after he became king! He had big plans. His pyramid would be the largest ever!

Egyptian fact!

Many poor people in Egypt died before the age of 35. Rich people lived about 10 years longer. We know this from scientific tests on skeletons.

Stargazing

The **pyramid** had to be in the right place. It must face north. If it did it was easier for the dead king to fly to the stars.

The king's **priest** used the stars to find north. First, he made a round wall of bricks. He stood inside the wall. He looked at the night sky.

The priest used the top of the wall as a guide. The priest looked through a forked stick. This helped him find the star he was looking for. He made marks on the wall. He marked the position of the star twice. He first marked it when it rose in the evening. Then he marked where the star set in the morning. North was halfway between the two marks.

The priest drew two lines in the sand. He drew one from each mark on the wall. He drew the lines until they met. He then drew a third line in the middle. This showed where north was.

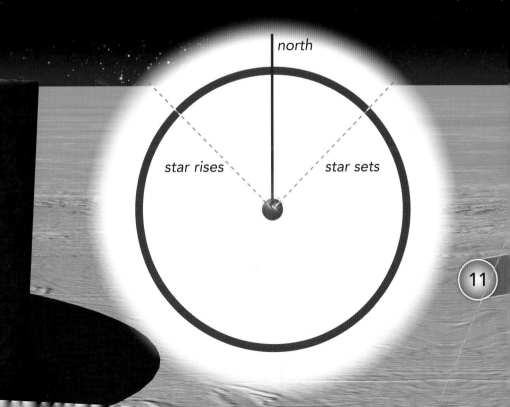

north

star rises

star sets

First stones

When the floods came, people could not work in the fields. They went to work for the king instead. They went to build the king's **pyramid**. This was where the king would be buried when he died.

The workers lived in a camp. The king visited them in his **chariot** (cart). He made **sacrifices** (offerings) of animals to the gods. He asked the gods for help.

Groups of 200 men were split into teams. Twenty men were in each team.

bent pyramid

perfect pyramid

chariot light cart with two wheels, pulled by horses
sacrifice offering to a god

How to build a pyramid

1. Check the stars. Make sure the pyramid faces north.
2. Set up camp.
3. Get tools from the tool store.
4. Mark out the base of the pyramid, with ropes.
5. Cut stones.
6. Start pulling stones into place.

step pyramid

These are the three types of pyramid. Khufu's father Sneferu built a pyramid with bent sides. The sides got bent because the builders changed the slope halfway.

Higher and higher

Stones came from a **quarry**. Workers made cuts with tools. They hammered wooden **wedges** (blocks of pointed wood) into the cuts. These wedges helped to split off blocks of stone.

It took between 10,000 and 20,000 people to build a **pyramid**. One big stone was as heavy as 200 men. Each stone was lifted on to a wooden sledge.

Scribes were able to write. They wrote down all the details of the building work.

quarry: place from where rock is cut

The builders made a ramp. They pulled stones up to the next level on the ramp.

Men pulled on ropes tied to the sledge. The sledge slid over sand on the ground.

The workers made a **ramp** of wet sand and rocks. They dragged stones up the sloping ramp. **Scribes** checked the work. Scribes were people who could write. They paid the workers. They were paid in loaves of bread each day.

Workers in camp

The days were very hot. Some workers got hurt. We know this from skeletons found at the camp. Crushed hands were common!

The Sun went down. Workers handed in their tools. The stars came out. It was cool. People cooked dinner.

Egyptians mostly ate bread, onions, and fruit. Egyptian bread tasted gritty. There was sand in the flour. Some days they had a barbecue of duck, beef, or lamb. They caught fish in the river. They made sweets out of honey.

After work, they sang songs and told stories. Sometimes they played games.

Crime and punishment

A worker who stole tools was punished. He was hit 100 times with a stick. He was cut five times. The scars showed he was a thief.

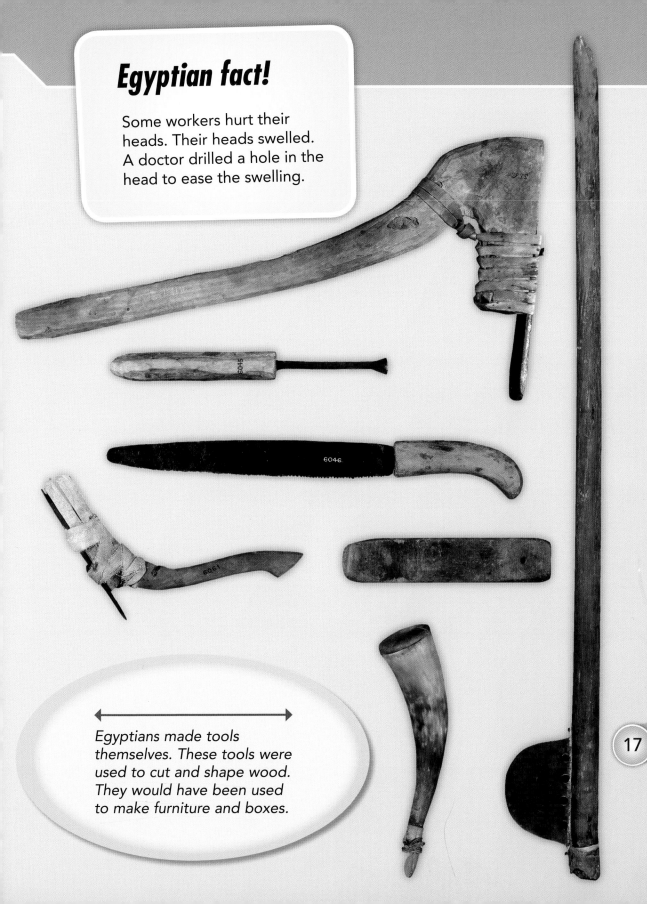

Egyptian fact!

Some workers hurt their heads. Their heads swelled. A doctor drilled a hole in the head to ease the swelling.

Egyptians made tools themselves. These tools were used to cut and shape wood. They would have been used to make furniture and boxes.

17

Temples and mysteries

King Khufu was pleased. The **pyramid** was getting taller. His new **temple** was nearly finished too.

Egypt had many temples. Inside each temple was a **statue** (a figure) of a god. Every morning, **priests** (religious leaders) washed the statue. They put food in front of it.

The Sphinx is a temple southwest of the Great Pyramid. It has a lion's body but a human's head.

funeral ceremony for a dead

Egyptian scribes wrote with pictures instead of words. This writing is called **hieroglyphics**. A scribe had to learn hundreds of pictures.

Kings liked big statues of themselves. Some statues weighed 1,000 tonnes.

Artists painted pictures on the walls of the new temple. **Scribes** (writers) wrote lists of the things King Khufu had done. The temple would be used for his **funeral**.

Secrets of the tomb

Khufu had been king for more than 10 years. The **pyramid** was now finished. The outside was covered with smooth white stones. It could be seen from far away. It looked like it was pointing to the stars.

Deep inside, workmen put in stone doors. The doors blocked tunnels. Only one tunnel led to the King's **tomb**. Inside was a stone **coffin**. Magic signs kept away evil. Outside, small pyramids were ready for the King's relatives.

This is the inside of the pyramid. Workmen scribbled Khufu's name inside the tomb. This is how we know it was his.

gallery

tunnel

air shaft

King's chamber

Queen's chamber

coffin – wooden or stone box for a dead body

Egyptians believed dead people needed food, furniture, and clothes. They put these things in tombs. A king was buried with treasure too. He wanted to look good in the **afterlife**.

Archaeologists *still study pyramids. They might find more treasures. Then we would understand more about how the ancient Egyptians lived.*

Making a mummy

Egyptians believed you could live again after you died. They believed you needed a body to live in the next world. They wanted to make sure the body did not rot away. They made it into a **mummy**.

The finished mummy often had a wooden face mask. Sometimes the mask was made of gold or bronze. It looked like the dead person. It was put in a **coffin**.

How to make a mummy

Firstly, the Egyptians took out the insides of the dead body. They hooked out the brain through the nose. Then they dried the body. They used salt and chemicals. The body was stuffed with rags. Then it was wrapped in cloth.

The good or bad test

The heart was left inside a mummy. Egyptians believed the gods weighed the heart. They also weighed a feather. A bad person's heart would weigh more than the feather. A monster named Ammit would then eat him.

Ramesses II was king of Egypt from 1304 to 1237 BC. This is his mummy. His mummy is more than 3,000 years old.

Egyptian fact!

It took 70 days to make a mummy. Each finger and toe was wrapped separately! Egyptians made mummies of cats and other animals too.

Stolen treasures

The **pyramid** was sealed (closed) after the king's body had been placed inside. The king would be buried with his treasure. The Egyptians believed they needed treasure in the **afterlife**. The afterlife was the place where people went after they died. Heavy stones slid into place to block the tunnels. The last workers climbed out into the fresh air. They hid the entrance.

Families went back to their villages. The pyramid was left to the sand and the stars. But thieves broke in. They stole the treasure. **Archaeologists** are people who find out about the past. When archaeologists went inside Khufu's pyramid, it was nearly empty.

Egyptian fact!

Archaeologists found a wooden boat in Khufu's pyramid. It was probably used at Khufu's **funeral**. It was in more than 1,000 pieces. They put it together again.

The Valley of the Kings

Later, kings built secret rock **tombs**. A tomb is a place where people are buried. The tombs were in the Valley of the Kings (see the map on page 5). One tomb was not robbed of all its treasures. It was opened in 1923. It belonged to a king called Tutankhamen.

These **statues** are made from gold. They were found in Tutankhamen's tomb. This was the place where he was buried.

Spooky!

Khufu's son Khaefre became king. His **pyramid** is almost as big as Khufu's.

The pyramids have stood for about 4,500 years. Their treasures have been stolen. Some have been taken to a museum. Some stones have also been stolen. People carried off stones to build houses.

This is Tutankhamen's **coffin**. Tutankhamen was a king who ruled about 3,300 years ago.

alien being from another world

↑ **Mummies** in films are scary. Real mummies interest scientists.

Pyramids can seem spooky. The French leader Napoleon went into Khufu's pyramid in 1799. He came out white-faced! He never said why. A few people think the pyramids were built by **aliens**! Nobody can be sure exactly how the pyramids were built. But they were made to stand forever, beneath the stars.

Fascinating facts!

Our word "**pyramid**" comes from a Greek word for "wheat cake". The pointy shape reminded the Greeks of a cake. Egyptians called a pyramid "mer".

Nathaniel Dawson tried to see inside the Great Pyramid. It was 1763. He was lowered inside on a rope. He had only a candle. None of his workmen would go in. The workmen were scared of ghosts!

The biggest stone in the Great Pyramid weighs 290 tonnes.

Egyptians measured in cubits. One cubit was the length of a man's arm from elbow to fingertip. This was about 45 centimetres (18 inches).

British explorer John Greaves crawled into Khufu's pyramid in the 1600s. All he found were bats!

Timeline

2650
Imhotep builds the first pyramid. It has "steps" not smooth sides. It is 60 metres (197 feet) high.

2600–2500
King Khufu builds the Great Pyramid at Giza. Two other large pyramids at Giza are built for King Khaefre and King Menkaure.

2181
End of the "Old Kingdom".

1938–1630
The time of the "Middle Kingdom".

1630–1520
Egyptians fight invaders called the Hyksos. The Hyksos take control of the north.

1570–1085
This is the time of the "New Kingdom". Egypt is strong again.

1352–1336
King Akhenaten starts a new religion. He worships just one god.

1333–1323
Tutankhamen is king.

332
Egypt is conquered by Alexander the Great. After him, Greek kings rule in Egypt.

69–30
Cleopatra is queen of Egypt. After her, Egypt is ruled by Rome.

AD

300s
The last pyramids. They are very small and made of brick.

Glossary

afterlife world of the dead. Egyptians believed that once they had died they joined the afterlife.

alien being from another world. One wild idea is that aliens from space built the pyramids!

archaeologist person who digs in the ground to find out about the past. Archaeologists help us to understand how pyramids were built.

chariot light cart with two wheels, pulled by horses. Wealthy ancient Egyptians travelled in chariots.

coffin wooden or stone box for a dead body. A king had several coffins, one inside the other.

crops plants grown for food. Some crops are wheat, barley, or corn.

funeral ceremony for a dead person. A king's funeral happened beside the River Nile.

hieroglyphics ancient Egyptian writing. Hieroglyphics are made up of pictures rather than words.

mummy dead body dried and wrapped to stop it rotting. Mummies were buried in coffins.

priest person who carries out religious duties. In ancient Egypt priests looked after temples.

pyramid solid shape with a square base and four triangular sides. Pyramids were special places where kings were buried.

quarry place from where rock is cut. A quarry can be a cliff or a deep hole.

ramp slope for moving things up and down. You might make a ramp from sand or dirt.

sacrifice offering to a god. People gave the gods food, drink, or a freshly killed animal as a sacrifice.

scribe person who could read and write. Scribes wrote for other people.

statue figure made from stone or metal. Kings often had statues made of themselves.

temple building in which people worship a god or gods. A priest was usually in charge in a temple.

tomb place in which dead people are buried. Pyramids were tombs for kings.

wedge block of pointed wood, used as a tool. A doorstop is a wedge.

Want to know more?

Books to read

Egyptian Myths and Legends, Fiona Macdonald (Raintree, 2013)

Everything Ancient Egypt, Crispin Boyer (National Geographic, 2012)

Mummies and Pyramids, Sam Taplin (Usborne, 2008)

The Awesome Egyptians (Horrible Histories), Terry Deary (Scholastic, 2007)

Websites

http://www.bbc.co.uk/history/ancient/egyptians/launch_gms_pyramid_builder.shtml
Visit this website to build your own pyramid!

http://www.childrensuniversity.manchester.ac.uk/interactives/history/egypt/
You can learn all about the ancient Egyptians on this website.

Read about ancient Rome in ***All About Life in Ancient Rome***.

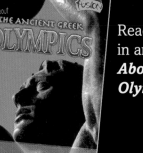

Read about the Olympics in ancient Greece in ***All About the Ancient Greek Olympics***.

Index